The Story of a Special Day
Volume 117

April
26

The 116th day of the year (117th in leap years). There are 249 days remaining until the end of the year.

by Michael Dobson

Timespinner
Press

This book is also available in e-book form for Kindle, e-pub devices, and other formats from your favorite online booksellers.

For more information about the series, about us, or about your special day, please email us at editor@timespinnerpress.com.

Look for other volumes in *The Story of a Special Day,* coming often. See www.timespinnerpress.com for details and for the most recent information.

Table of Contents

Cover: The "Chandos portrait" of William Shakespeare, from the National Portrait Gallery, London. William Shakespeare was baptised April 26, 1564 — the COVER STORY and PERSON OF THE DAY.

Quote of the Day

"If people did not sometimes do silly things, nothing intelligent would ever get done."

Ludwig Wittgenstein, philosopher
born April 26, 1889

Today
in
History

April 26

Chernobyl: Last Day of Pripyat, Alexey Akindinov (CC BY-SA 4.0)

What Happened on April 26?

Event of the Day
Chernobyl Disaster (1986)

On April 26, 1986, a reactor at the Chernobyl Nuclear Power Plant (then in the Soviet Union, now in the Ukraine) suffered a catastrophic failure. It is one of only two nuclear energy accidents classified as "Level 7," and is overall the most disastrous nuclear power plant accident in history.

The event occurred during a late night safety test in which safety systems were deliverately turned off. A conbination of design flaws in the reactor and failure to follow the checklist on the part of the operators resulted in an uncontrolled reaction that led to a steam explosion, scattering radioactive material throughout the western USSR and Europe.

Immediate casualties included 2 deaths and 134 hospitalized with radiation poisoning; of them, at least 28 died within a few months. After some delay, nearby towns were evacuated. Numerous cancer deaths resulted, with nearly 5 percent of the population suffering measurable effectss

A massive cleanup effort that lasted seven months resulted in a massive concrete sarcophagus encasing the remains of the reactor. The financial effects were enormous, and played a part in the failure of the Soviet Union a few years later. Nearly 4 million acres of agricultural and forest land were taken out of production. While some of the area has been returned to cultivation, parts will not be safe for human life for another 20,000 years.

From the creation of great works of engineering and art, to devastating wars and natural disasters, thousands of years of history have left their mark on each and every day of the year. Here are some additional important events that occurred on April 26. (Illustrated items are shaded.)

1777 — Although the truth of this story is somewhat clouded, **Abigail Ludington,** age 16, rode her horse through the night to alert colonial militia in New York and Connecticut that **the British were coming,** and became a heroine of the American Revolution.

1803 — A shower of more than 3,000 stones falls on the town of L'Aigle in Normandy, France, **proving the existence of meteors and meteorites**.

1865 — US Army troopers shoot and kill Lincoln assassin **John Wilkes Booth**.

1933 — The Nazi government in Germany establishes a secret police force, the **Gestapo.**

1937 — During the Spanish Civil War, German Luftwaffe bomb the city of **Guernica**. The bombing is commemorated in a famous painting by Picasso.

1962 — NASA's Ranger 4 spacecraft **crashes into the Moon**, the first US object to reach another celestial body.

1989 — The **deadliest tornado in recorded history** strikes central Bangladesh, killing over 1,300 and leaving 80,000 homeless.

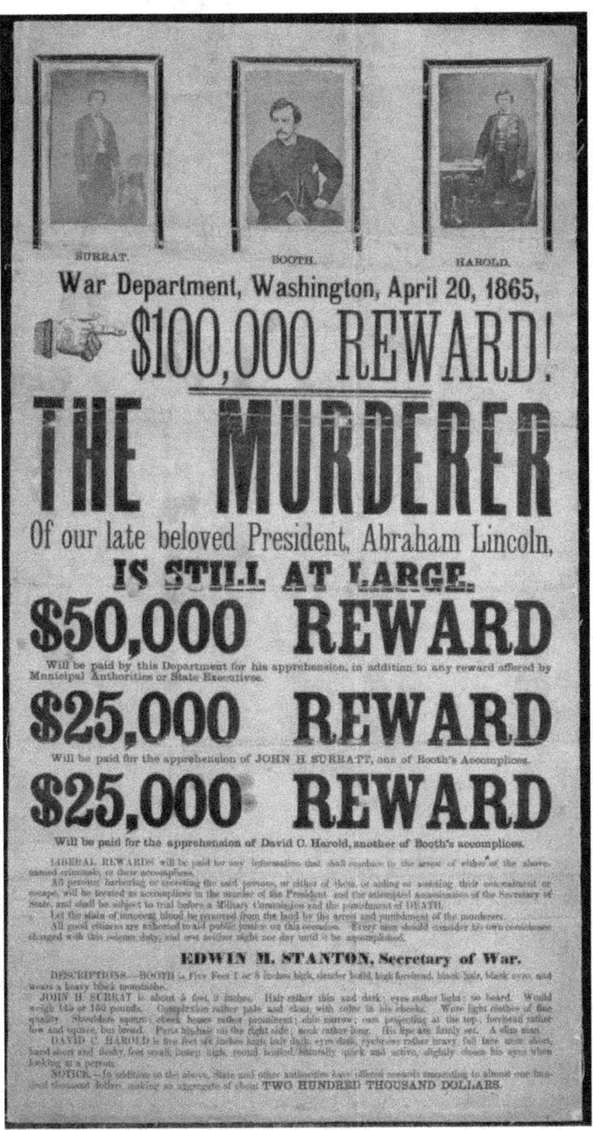

Wanted poster for Lincoln assassin John Wilkes Booth

Quote of the Day

"All is ephemeral — fame and the famous
as well."

Marcus Aurelius, Roman emperor
and Stoic philosopher
born April 26, 121

Births
and
Deaths

THERIACA MAGNA

April 26

John James Audubon, by John Syme (Courtesy White House). Audubon, known for his detailed illustrations of American birds, was born April 26, 1785.

Notable April 26 People

With the current world population at about seven billion people, on average about 19 million people also celebrate their birthdays on April 26 — and that isn't counting the millions and millions who came before! No matter when you were born, you share your birthday with many special people whose accomplishments (and occasionally embarrassments) have been noted as part of history.

In this section, you'll meet fascinating people who share your birthday. They're organized by what they're famous for, and then in reverse chronological order from most recent to earliest. Those who are shown in photographs or artwork have a box around them. We don't have photos of everyone, so please forgive us if your favorite person is missing.

Some of these people you've heard of, others may be new to you, but they all make up an important part of the reason that April 26 is a truly special day!

Cover of Shakespeare's "First Folio," published 1623

Who Was Born on April 26?

Cover Story/Person of the Day
William Shakespeare (1564*)

Poet, playwright, and actor, William Shakespeare is widely thought of as the greatest writer in the English language. His known works include 38 plays, 154 sonnets, and two long narrative poems. A few additional works may be by Shakespeare, but the authorship is not confirmed.

Born and raised in the town of Stratford-upon-Avon, Shakespeare probably attended the nearby King's New School, a "grammar school." At the time, a grammar school taught Latin and was closer to a modern secondary school.

Shakespeare married Anne Hathaway when he was 18 years old. The couple had three children, a daughter, Susanna (born six months after the wedding), and fraternal twins Hamnet and Judith. Hamnet, his only son, died at the age of 11.

At some point after the birth of his twins, Shakespeare moved to London, where he became part of the London theatrical scene. His life during the so-called "lost years" between 1585 and 1592 is unknown, though there are a number of theories.

---

* The actual date of Shakepeare's birth is unknown, but the date of his baptism, April 26, 1564, is recorded. The baptismal date was considered more important at that time than the birthday.

By 1592, when Shakespeare was 28 years old, several of his plays had been produced on the London stage. He was better known as an actor, appearing in a number of plays by Ben Jonson, among others.

He soon became a partner in a theatrical company called the Lord Chamberlain's Men, later the King's Men, chartered by King James VI and I, following the death of Queen Elizabeth I. In 1599, the partnership built their own theater, the Globe, making Shakespeare a wealthy man. He bought a large house in Stratford, and divided his time between London and Stratford.

Shakespeare's Globe Theater modern reconstruction (Photo: Peter Broster, CC BY-SA 2.0). The original Globe Theater burned down in 1613; a second was built the following year and lasted until 1642.

Although he was popular both as an actor and a playwright, he was not well thought of by some critics. One called him an "upstart crow," daring to think himself as good as such university-educated writers as Christopher Marlowe.

Shakespeare, by William Blake (1800)

Nevertheless, by the early 1590s, Shakespeare had already written the historical dramas *Richard III* and the three parts of *Henry VI*, as well as *The Comedy of Errors* and *The Taming of the Shrew*.

A series of romantic comedies followed, including *A Midsummer Night's Dream* and *Much Ado About Nothing*. Shakespeare next turned to tragedy, with *Romeo and Juliet, Julius Caesar, Hamlet, King Lear,* and *Macbeth*. In the later part of his career he wrote *The Tempest*, and collaborated on a few additional works. Much of his poetry was written during an outbreak of plague in London in 1593 and 1594, when theaters were closed for fear of disease, although he wrote sonnets for his friends throughout his life.

Shakespeare died April 23, 1616, at the age of 52. Most of his estate went to his daughter Susanna. His wife Anne famously received his "second best bed." This may have been an insult, or it may have referred to their matrimonial bed. He was buried at the Holy Trinity Church in Stratford-upon-Avon.

Plays at the time were generally ephemeral, and aside from a few flimsy "quarto" editions of individual plays, his work was not collected during his lifetime. However, in 1632, two of Shakespeare's friends published a collection known to scholars as the "First Folio." Some of the plays in the First Folio differ substantially from their earlier quarto versions, and scholars still debate which version is most faithful.

Although well liked and popular during his lifetime, Shakespeare's reputation grew after his death, and by the 19th century, the "Bard of Avon" had achieved his modern reputation as the great genius of English letters. His work continues to be adapted and produced in many media.

The actress Sarah Bernhardt as Hamlet, 1899

Art and Architecture

I. M. Pei, architect known for such buildings as the National Gallery East Building, the Louvre "glass pyramid," and many other buildings; received the Pritzker Prize, sometimes call the Nobel Prize of architecture. *(1917)*

Edmund C. Tarbell, American Impressionist painter known as one of the "Ten American Painters." *(1862)*

Frederick Law Olmstead, "father of American landscape architecture," best known for designing New York's Central Park and San Francisco's Golden Gate Park. *(1822)*

New York's Central Park (Photo: Gigi Alt, CC BY-SA 3.0)

Eugène Delacroix, French Romantic painter who influenced the Impressionist and Symbolist movements. *(1798)*

John James Audubon, American ornithologist and painter noted for his detailed and accurate illustrations of birds, compiled in his classic work *The Birds of America. (1785)*

Three canvas-backed ducks (*Nyroca valisineria*), John James Audubon (1827). Courtesy Wellcome Images

Business

James Rouse, American real estate developer and urban planner best known for his "planned community" of Columbia, Maryland. *(1914)*

Government

Melania Trump, fashion model and First Lady to US President Donald Trump. *(1970)*

Rudolf Hess, Nazi politician and deputy führer to Adolf Hitler, famous for his flight to Scotland to try to negotiate peace with the United Kingdom. *(1894)*

Marcus Aurelius, emperor of Rome from 161 to 180; last of the "Five Good Emperors;" also known for his writing about Stoic philosophy. *(121)*

Bust of Marcus Aurelius (Photo: Bibi Saint-Pol)

Journalism and Literature

Morris West, novelist and playwright best known for his 1963 work *The Shoes of the Fisherman,* adapted into a successful film. *(1916)*

Bernard Malamud, best-selling American novelist known for *The Natural* and *The Fixer,* both adapted into film. *(1914)*

A. E. van Vogt, science fiction writer considered one of the most influential creators (along with Robert Heinlein and Isaac Asimov) during science fiction's Golden Age. *(1912)*

Vicente Aleixandre, Spanish poet who received the 1977 Nobel Prize for Literature, considered one of the greatest poets in that language. *(1898)*

Anita Loos, American screenwriter and novelist best known for her 1925 best-seller *Gentlemen Prefer Blondes,* made into a Broadway musical and a hit film starring Marilyn Monroe and Jane Russell. *(1889)*

Artemus Ward, American humor writer considered to be the nation's first stand-up comedian. *(1822)*

Military and Adventure

Jessica Lynch, American soldier injured and captured by Iraqi forces; her recovery by US special forces was the first successful rescue of an American POW since Vietnam. *(1983)*

Samantha Cristoforetti, Italian air force pilot and engineer who became the first Italian woman in space; set a record for the longest single space flight by a woman and as the first person to brew an espresso in space. *(1977)*

Ernst Udet, German flying ace during World War I and an air force general during World War II. *(1896)*

Music

Gary Wright, singer-songwriter best known for "Dream Weaver." *(1943)*

Bobby Rydell, singer best known for his hits "Wild One" and "Volare." *(1942)*

Giorgio Moroder, singer-songwriter and record producer known for producing such hits as "Last Dance," "MacArthur Park," "Here She Comes," "Take My Breath Away, and "Flashdance." Won the Academy Award for Best Original Song twice. *(1940)*

Duane Eddy, guitarist known for such hits as "Rebel Rouser," "Peter Gunn," and "Because They're Young;" inducted into the Rock and Roll Hall of Fame. *(1938)*

Ma Rainey, one of the earliest African-American professional blues singers and one of the first to make a record; billed as the "mother of the blues." *(1886[†])*

[†] Some sources say September 1882.

Bobby Rydell

Ma Rainey

Performing Arts

Channing Tatum, actor who starred in such films as *Magic Mike, 21 Jump Street,* and *White House Down.* *(1980)*

Jordana Brewster, actress and model best known for her role as Mia in the *Fast and Furious* films. *(1980)*

Stana Katic, actress best known for playing Kate Beckett on the TV series *Castle.* *(1978)*

Tom Welling, actor best known as Clark Kent/ Superboy in the 2001 series *Smallville.* *(1977)*

Jet Li, actor and martial artist whose films include *Lethal Weapon 4, The Expendables,* and *The Mummy: Tomb of the Dragon Emperor.* *(1963)*

Michael Damian, actor best known for his role as Danny Romalotti on *The Young and the Restless* over a three decade period. *(1962)*

Joan Chen, actress known for roles in *The Last Emperor, Twin Peaks,* and other films. *(1961)*

Giancarlo Esposito, actor best known for his roles on the TV series *Breaking Bad* and *Better Call Saul,* along with roles in numerous Spike Lee films. *(1958)*

Koo Stark, British actress and model best known for her relationship with Prince Andrew. *(1956)*

Claudine Auger, model and acress best known as "Bond girl" Domino Derval in 1965's *Thunderball.* *(1941)*

Carol Burnett, actress and comedienne best known for *The Carol Burnett Show. (1933)*

Carol Burnett

Bernie Brillstein, producer of television shows including *Hee Haw, The Muppet Show,* and *The Sopranos,* and films including *The Blues Brothers, Ghostbusters,* and *Happy Gilmore. (1931)*

Tomoyuki Tanaka (田中 友幸), Japanese film producer best known for co-creating Godzilla. *(1910)*

Theatrical release poster for *Godzilla* (1954)

Religion and Philosophy

Ludwig Wittgenstein, philosopher noted for work in logic, mathematics, thought, and language. *(1889)*

Science and Technology

Arno Allan Penzias, shared the 1978 Nobel Prize in Physics as co-discoverer of cosmic microwave background radiation. *(1933)*

Michael Smith, shared the 1993 Nobel Prize in Chemistry for his work in developing site-directed mutagenesis. *(1932)*

Charles Richter, seismologist and physicist who created the Richter magnitude scale to quantify the size of earthquakes. *(1900)*

Sir Owen Richardson, received the 1928 Nobel Prize in Physics for his work on thermionic emission. *(1879)*

Sports

Bill Wennington, basketball player for the Chicago Bulls; represented Canada in the 1984 Olympics; member of the Canadian Basketball Hall of Fame. *(1963)*

Harry "the Horse" Gallatin, basketball player and coach named to the Naismith Memorial Basketball Hall of Fame and the National Collegiate Basketball Hall of Fame. *(1927) (Photo next page.)*

Browning Ross, American long-distance runner credited with making the sport popular in the United States. *(1924)*

Harry Gallatin

Fanny Blankers-Koen, Dutch athlete nicknamed "the Flying Housewife," who won four gold medals in track at the 1948 Summer Olympics. *(1918)*

Sal Maglie, baseball pitcher best known as the only pitcher to play for all three New York baseball teams then active in the city; nicknamed "Sal the Barber." *(1917)*

Hack Wilson, baseball power hitter for 12 seasons in major league baseball; inducted into the Baseball Hall of Fame. *(1900)*

Eddie Eagan, only person to ever win an Olympic gold medal in both the Summer (boxing) and Winter games (bobsledding) in different events. *(1898)*

Eddie Eagan

Count Basie (Photo: William Gottlieb)

Who Died on April 26?

Crime and Punishment

John Wilkes Booth, actor and assassin of Abraham Lincoln. *(1865) (Photo and additional text on pages 4 and 5.)*

Journalism and Literature

A. B. Guthrie Jr., novelist and screenwriter who won the 1950 Pulitzer Prize in Fiction for his novel *The Way West. (1991)*

Armstrong Sperry, writer and illustrator of children's books, best known for his Newberry Medal-winning 1941 book *Call It Courage. (1976)*

Bjørnstjerne Bjørnson, Norwegian poet who received the 1903 Nobel Prize in Literature. *(1910)*

Music

George Jones, country musician and singer-songwriter best known for "He Stopped Loving Her Today." *(2013)*

Phoebe Snow, singer-songwriter best known for her 1975 hit "Poetry Man." *(2011)*

Carmine Coppola, composer best known for his original music for the *Godfather* films, directed by his son Francis Ford Coppola. *(1991)*

Leo Arnaud, composer whose song "Bugler's Dream" is used as the theme for US networks presenting the Olympic Games. *(1991)*

Count Basie, influential jazz pianist and bandleader for more than half a century; member of the Grammy Hall of Fame. *(1984) (Photo page 26.)*

Performing Arts

Jonathan Demme, director and producer of such films as *Swing Shift, Stop Making Sense, The Silence of the Lambs,* and *Philadelphia. (2017)*

Jayne Meadows, actress and sister of Audrey Meadows and wife of Steve Allen, best known as a panelist on *I've Got a Secret* and other game shows. *(1991)*

Jack Valenti, president of the Motion Picture Association of America, created the MPAA film rating system. *(2007)*

Emily McLaughlin, actress who played Nurse Jessie Brewer on the daytime drama *General Hospital. (1991)*

Lucille Ball, actress, producer, and studio executive best known for her sitcom *I Love Lucy. (1989)*

Broderick Crawford, actor best known for his roles in the 1949 film *All the King's Men* and the 1950s television series *Highway Patrol. (1986)*

Jim Davis, actor best known as Jock Ewing in the prime-time soap opera *Dallas. (1981)*

Lucille Ball (right) with Desi Arnaz in *I Love Lucy* (1956)

Irene Ryan, actress best remembered for her role as Granny on *The Beverly Hillbillies. (1973)*

Gypsy Rose Lee, actress, author, and burlesque entertainer famous for her striptease act; her memoir was turned into the stage and screen musical *Gypsy. (1970)*

Science

Carl Bosch, chemist and engineer who founded IG Farben, which became the world's largest chemical company for a time; received the 1931 Nobel Prize in Chemistry for his achievements in high-pressure industrial chemistry. *(1940)*

Sports

Marcel Pronovost, hockey player with the Detroit Red Wings and the Toronto Maple Leafs for twenty years; member of the Hockey Hall of Fame. *(2015)*

Masutatsu Ōyama (大山 倍達), founded Kyokushin Karate, a full-contact karate style. *(1994)*

Gichin Funakoshi (船越 義珍), founded Shotokan Karate-Do; known as the "father of modern karate." *(1957)*

Irene Ryan

Gypsy Rose Lee (Credit: Los Angeles *Times)*

$\mathfrak{Q}$uote of the $\mathfrak{D}$ay

"If a thing is worth doing, it's worth doing slowly...very slowly."

Gypsy Rose Lee, ecdysiast and author
died April 26, 1970

Holidays
Around
the World
April 26

                                    Michael Dobson

La crucifixión by El Greco

April 26 Holidays and Celebrations

If you're looking for a reason to take your special day off, you should know that every single day is a holiday somewhere in the world! Here's some of what you can celebrate on April 26!

Easter Season

The Christian holiday of Easter in Western Christianity is held on the first Sunday after the Paschal Full Moon following the March equinox, which is officially set at March 21 by church reckoning. In Western Christianity, Easter itself can therefore occur as early as March 22 and as late as April 25, but occurs most often in April.

In Eastern Christianity, which uses the Julian calendar, Easter occurs between April 4 and May 8. This also sets the date for the various events that lead up to Easter, especially the events of Holy Week.

Passion Sunday

The fifth Sunday of the Christian season of Lent is known as Passion Sunday in various Protestant denominations and by some traditionalist Catholics. Sometimes, the sixth Sunday of Lent is referred to as Passion Sunday, but it is more commonly known as Palm Sunday.

Passion Sunday starts the two-week Passiontide, which ends on Holy Saturday, the day before Easter, commemorating the day that Jesus's body was laid in the tomb.

Palm Sunday

The moveable feast of Palm Sunday commemorates the triumphant entry of Jesus into Jerusalem, an event mentioned in all four gospels. In many Christian churches, palm leaves are distributed to the worshippers.

Maundy Thursday

The Thursday before Easter is Maundy Thursday, when the Last Supper took place.

Good Friday

Good Friday, observed during Holy Week on the Friday preceding Easter Sunday, commemorates the crucifixion of Jesus and his death at Calvary.

Holy Saturday

Sometimes called Easter Eve or Black Saturday, Holy Saturday commemorates the day in which Jesus's body lay in the tomb. Some mistakenly refer to this day as "Easter Saturday," but that properly describes the Saturday following Easter, the last day of Easter Week. The earliest it can occur is March 21, and the latest is April 24.

Easter

Easter celebrates the resurrection of Jesus Christ on the third day after his crucifixion.

Easter Eggs

In the liturgical calendar, Easter follows the season of Lent, and begins the period known as Eastertide, which ends on Pentecost Sunday. Easter is observed religiously in a morning service.

In the U.S., it's also common to decorate Easter eggs and make Easter baskets of eggs and candy, often with the Easter bunny as a symbol. The White House traditionally hosts an egg hunt, and many communities have Easter parades.

Easter customs around the world include bonfires (Cyprus, western Sweden), men spanking women with a ceremonial whip (Czech Republic and Slovakia), egg fighting (Bulgaria), cross-country skiing and reading murder mysteries (Norway), and children dressed as witches collecting candy door-to-door (other Nordic countries).

Easter Monday

In some Roman Catholic and Eastern Orthodox cultures, the Monday after Easter is celebrated as a holiday.

It is also known in some countries as **Egg Nyte**, featuring egg rolling competitions and dousing other people with water that had been blessed with holy water the previous day at mass.

Easter Monday is also celebrated as **Family Day** in South Africa. In Guyana, people fly kites that were made on Holy Saturday. In Portugal, it is known as the **Anjo (Ivy) Festival**, in which people picnic in the countryside.

Śmigus-Dyngus (Poland, Hungary, Czech Republic, Slovakia)

The Monday after Easter in Poland and in the Polish diaspora is known as *Śmigus-Dyngus,* or simply Dyngus Day in the US. Boys throw water over girls they like and spank them with pussy willows. Girls avoid getting wet by giving boys "ransoms" of painted eggs.

Easter Week (Western Christianity)/Bright Week (Eastern Christianity)

The period from Easter Sunday to the following Saturday is known as **Easter Week** in Western Christianity and **Bright Week** in Eastern Christianity. **Easter Tuesday** is a public holiday in the Australian state of Tasmania. Because of the difference in the calculation of the date of Easter, Easter Week and Bright Week happen on different weeks each year.

A Bright Week procession

Other Religious Feast Days and Holidays

Passover (פסח) (Judaism, Samaritanism, Saint Thomas Christians)

Passover commemorates the liberation of the Israelites from slavery in ancient Egypt around 3,300 years ago. Its story is told in the Biblical book of Exodus, which is part of both the Jewish and Samaritan Torahs and the Christian Old Testament. Exodus tells how God inflicted ten plagues upon the ancient Egyptians before the Pharaoh would release its slaves. The tenth plague killed every Egyptian first-born child. Israelites marked the doorposts of their homes with the blood of a spring lamb so that the spirit of the Lord would "pass over" the first-born in those homes.

Passover is celebrated by Jews in a festive ritual dinner known as a Seder and by Samaritans with an animal sacrifice on Mount Gerizim.

For most celebrants, Passover begins on the 15th day of Nisan and ends on the 21st of Nisan in Israel and on the 22nd of Nisan outside of Israel. The earliest dates for Passover are between March 21 and March 27 (or 28), and the latest dates fall between April 20 and April 26 (or 27).

The First Passover Feast, by Huybrecht Beuckelaer

Saint Days

Each day in the year is considered a feast day for one or more saints. They are somewhat different in western Christianity (Catholicism and many forms of Protestantism) and in eastern (Orthodox) Christianity. There are many others; this is a selection.

In *Western Christianity*, April 26 is the feast day of Aldobrandesca, Franca Visalta, Lucidus of Verona, Our Lady of Good Counsel, Popes Anacletus and Marcellinus, Riquier, Paschasius Radbertus, Peter of Rates, Robert Hunt (Episcopal Church USA), Stephen of Perm, and Trudpert.

In *Eastern Orthodox Christianity*, it is also the commemoration of Saints Andrew and Anatolius, Justa, Leo of Samos, Exuperantia, Clarentius, and Richarius. (These saints are honored on April 13 by "Old Calendrists.‡")

General Events

Confederate Memorial Day (Florida, Georgia)

Several states in the American South observe a Confederate Memorial Day, not all on the same day. In Florida and Georgia, it is commemorated on April 26.

---

‡ "Old Calendrists" use the older Julian calendar rather than the modern Gregorian calendar for liturgical purposes. April 13 on the Julian calendar is the same day as March 31 on the Gregorian calendar. For more about the different types of calendars, see "What Day of the Week is April 13?"

Old Permic Alphabet Day (parts of eastern Russia)

Saint Stephen of Perm, a Russian missionary, developed a writing system for the Komi (eastern Russian peoples) language, known as the Permic alphabet. It is the second oldest writing system for an Uralic language. In the 17th century, it gave way to the Cyrillic script. Saint Stephen of Perm's feast day is also commemorated as Old Permic Alphabet Day

Union Day (Tanzania)

Tanzania was created from a merger of Tanganyika and Zanzibar on April 26, 1964.

World Intellectual Property Day (international)

Established by the World Intellectual Property Organization, this day raises awarness of how patents, copyrights, trademarks, and designs impact daily life. It takes place on the anniversary of the 1970 founding of the organization.

Food Holidays

In the United States, almost every day of the year is dedicated to a particular food — some days honor more than one!. (Other countries also have official food days, but not one for each day.) Sponsored by manufacturers, retailers, farmers, or simply fans, these days are often proclaimed by the President, Congress, state governors, or mayors.

In the US, April 26 is **National Pretzel Day.** Prezels were invented in 610 CE by a monk who lived in southern France or northern Italy. It migrated first to Germany, where it acquired its name. The hard pretzel was invented in Lancaster County, Pennsylvania, around 1710.

German children once wore pretzel necklaces to mark the new year. Pretzels were also known as a "marriage knot," and as part of 17th century wedding ceremonies, the couple would wish upon a pretzel, break it, and eat the pieces — from which we get the expression "tying the knot."

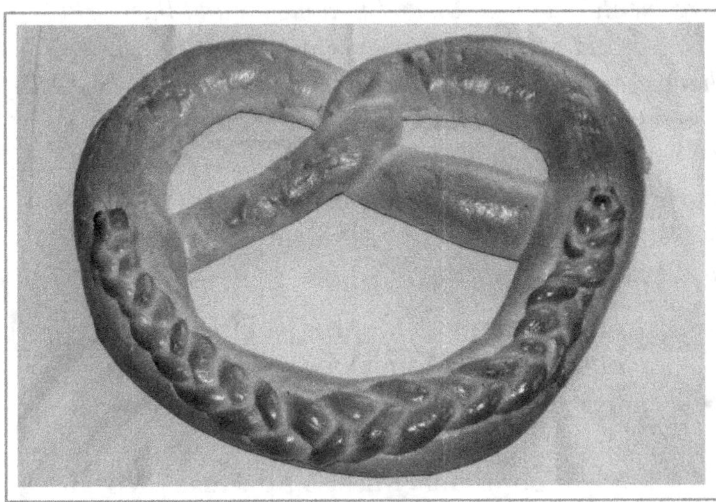

A New Year's pretzel (Photo: Rosenzweig, CC BY-SA 3.0)

Honorary Food Months: *In addition, the entire month of April is used to celebrate numerous foods. Here's a list of food-related observances in the month of April!*

- National Florida Tomato Month
- National BLT Sandwich Month
- National Pecan Month
- National Soft Pretzel Month
- National Soyfoods Month
- National Grilled Cheese Month
- National Garlic Month

Honorary Months

Presidents, Congresses, and nations around the world issue proclamations recognizing particular months to honor certain causes. These events generally fall in April, though honorary months do come and go.

Two places to get up to date information are the current edition of Chase's Calendar of Events or the website Brownielocks. Here are some honorary designations for April.

- Alcohol Awareness Month (National Council on Alcoholism and Drug Dependence)
- Cancer Control Month
- Confederate History Month (Alabama, Florida, Georgia, Louisiana, Mississippi, Texas, Virginia)
- Earthquake Preparedness Month (California)
- Fair Housing Month
- Grange Month (National Grange)

- Holy Humor Month (Fellowship of Merry Christians)
- International Guitar Month
- Jazz Appreciation Month (Smithsonian Institution)
- Month of the Young Child® (Michigan Association for the Education of Young Children)
- National Arab-American Heritage Month
- National Autism Awareness Month (Autism Society of America)
- National Car Care Month (Car Care Council)
- National Child Abuse Prevention Month
- National Donate Life Month (Organ donations)
- National Frog Month
- National Greyhound Adoption Month
- National Kite Month (American Kiteflyers Association)
- National Landscape Architecture Month (American Society of Landscape Architects)
- National Poetry Month (Academy of American Poets)
- National Poetry Writing Month (NaPoWriMo)
- National Youth Sports Safety Month (National Youth Sports Safety Foundation)
- Parkinson's Disease Awareness Month (International)
- Prevention of Animal Cruelty Month (ASPCA)
- School Library Media Month (American Library Association)
- Sexual Assault Awareness and Prevention Month (National Sexual Violence Resource Center)

- Sports Eye Safety Month (American Academy of Ophthalmology)
- Straw Hat Month

Moveable and Multi-Day Events

Some events take place over a specific week or time period. Start and finish dates may vary from year to year. Some events occur on different days each year (such as "fourth Saturday of a month"). These events sometimes take place on or include April 26.

Last Week in April

- Administrative Professionals Week
- National Princess Week
- National Volunteer Week
- Sky Awareness Week
- National Playground Safety Week
- National Scoop the Poop Week
- World Immunization Week

Just for Fun

Anybody can make up a holiday, and many people do! While none of these are officially recognized and some may come and go, here are a few more holidays for April 26.

- National Golf Day
- Hug an Australian Day
- Lesbian Visibility Day
- Richter Scale Day

"April" by Eugène Grasset

Quote of the Day

"Oh, the lovely fickleness of an
April day!"

W. H. Gibson, *Pastoral Days*

51

 Michael Dobson

"April," from the *Brevarium Grimani* by Simon Bening (c.1510)

April: The Fourth Month

*"I love the season well
When forest glades are teeming with bright forms,
Nor dark and many-folded clouds foretell
The coming on of storms."*

— *"An April Day," Henry Wadsworth Longfellow*

The origin of the name "April" (Latin: Aprilis) for the fourth month of the year is uncertain. Some say that it comes from the Latin verb aperire, meaning "to open," a reference to springtime. A similar word in Greek, άνοιξις (*anoixis*), meaning "opening" also refers to spring.

On the other hand, the Romans named many months after their gods, such as "January" for Janus and "March" (*Martius*) for Mars. The month of April was sacred to the goddess Venus (Aphrodite in Greek), and thus some think that April refers to her.

The fairy tale collector Jacob Grimm suggested that April came from the Etruscan name *Apru*, and believed that an Etruscan god or hero of that name gave rise to the month.

As the original Roman calendar started its new year in March, April was originally the second month of the year. It's uncertain when the Romans switched the new year to January, but it may have been as late as 153 BCE.

April is the springtime month in the northern hemisphere and fall in the southern hemisphere;

October is its opposite. It's one of only four calendar months with thirty days. Originally, April had only 29 days, but the calendar reforms of Julius Caesar (the Julian calendar[§]) added the 30th day.

The first day of April and the first day of July always fall on the same day of the week; in leap years the first of January also falls on the same weekday as the first of April. In all years, the last day of April and the last day of December fall on the same weekday.

April in Other Cultures

The month of April has different names in different languages. Some nations use calendars other than the Gregorian, and their months may overlap with April. Still, they often have a word for April itself.

Albanian: Prill

Arabic (Egypt, Sudan, Yemen): مارأبريل (Abrīl)

Belarussian: красавік (Krasavik)

Bulgarian: април (April)

Chinese (Mandarin): 四月 (Sìyuè)

Croatian: Travanj

Czech: Duben

Finnish: Huhtikuu (burnwood month)

French: Avril

Greek: Απρίλιος (Aprílios)

[§] . For more about the different types of calendars, see "What Day of the Week is April 13?

Hebrew: אפריל (Âprîl)

Hindi: अप्रैल (Aprail)

Irish (Gaelic): Aibreán mí Aibreáin

Italian: Aprile

Japanese: 四月 (Shigatsu)

Korean: 사월 (Saweol)

Lithuanian: Balandis

Old English: Ēastermōnaþ

Polish: Kwiecieńc

Russian: апрель (Aprel')

Scots: Apryle

Scottish Gaelic: an Giblean

Swahili: Aprili

Thai: เมษายน (Mesayon)

Ukrainian: квітень (Kviten')

Vietnamese: Tháng tư

April Sayings and Superstitions

Here are some sayings and superstitions associated with the month of April.

"April showers bring May flowers."

"If early April is foggy / Rain in June will make lanes boggy."

"When April blows its horn / 'Tis good for hay and corn."

"April wet — good wheat."

"Till April's dead, change not a thread."

"Marry in May and rue the day, but marry in April if you can, joy for maiden and for man." Which day? "Monday for wealth, Tuesday for health, Wednesday the best day of all, Thursday for losses, Friday for crosses, Saturday for no luck at all."

April Symbols

Birthstone: Diamond

Birth Flowers: Daisy and Sweet Pea

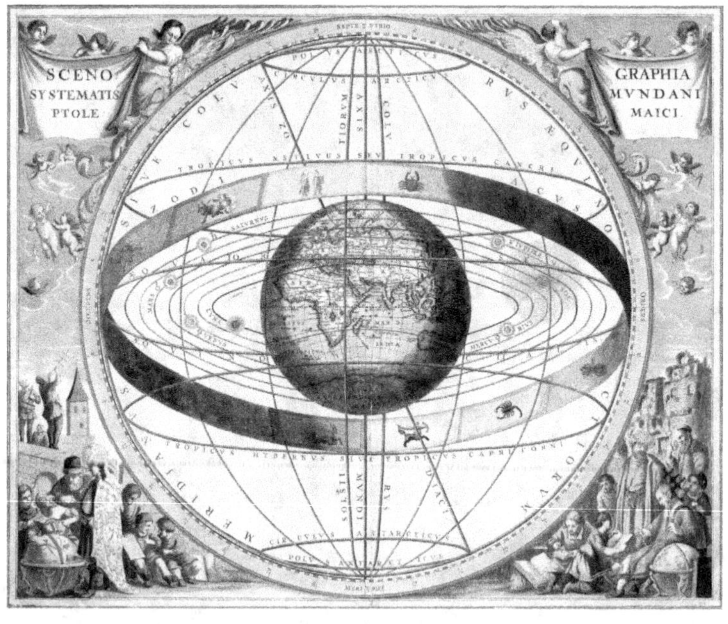

Scenography of the Ptolemaic Cosmography, by Johannes van Loon, based on Andreas Cellarius's *Harmonia Macrocosmica,* 1660

April 26 Zodiac Signs

From the perspective of someone on Earth, the Sun appears to move through the sky throughout the year, along a path astronomers call the *ecliptic plane*. The ecliptic plane is divided into twelve constellations, known as the zodiac, based on traditionally observed patterns of stars. On your birthday, you can't see your constellation, because it's in the daytime sky.

The zodiac was first developed by Babylonian astronomers about 2,500 years ago. Because they were unaware that the Earth wobbles like a spinning top (known as *precession*), they didn't make allowance for the fact that the Sun's path through the zodiac changes over time.

That means there are now two sets of dates for your birth sign. The *tropical dates* are the original Babylonian dates; the *sidereal dates* tell you where the Sun actually appears as it moves along its annual path.

For April 26, the tropical sign is **Taurus** and the sidereal sign is **Aries.**

 Michael Dobson

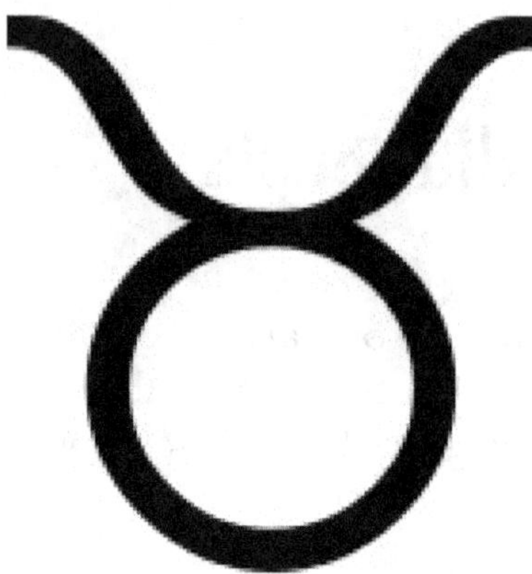

Taurus

Tropical April 21 to May 21
Sidereal May 16 to June 15

The astrological sign of Taurus (the Bull) originated in ancient Mesopotamia, who called it the "Bull of Heaven," and believed it to be a symbol of strong will, perseverance, and determination. The Egyptians knew it as Hathor (the Cow Goddess), who was the goddess of beauty, love, and happiness. That's why Roman astrologers said that Taurus was ruled by Venus, their goddess of beauty.

In astrology, Taurus is an Earth sign, compatible with Cancer, Capricorn, and Pisces. Taureans are supposed to be headstrong, powerful, and hard-working.

Aries

Tropical March 21 to April 19
Sidereal April 15 to May 15

In Greek mythology, Aries is a ram with golden wings and golden wool who rescued the twins Phrixus and Helle from certain death. Although Helle died in the rescue attempt, the grateful Phrixus sacrificed the ram to Zeus. The golden fleece from the sacrificed ram played a prominent part in the later myth of Jason and the Argonauts.

In astrology, Aries, a fire sign, is compatible with the other fire signs of Gemini, Leo, and Sagittarius, and to a lesser extent with air signs Scorpio and Libra. Arians are supposed to be adventurous, enthusiastic, quick-tempered, and impulsive.

Illustration by Edward Penfield

What Day of the Week is April 26?

On what day of the week does April 26 fall?

Surprisingly, this isn't an easy question. Because the calendar year is 365 days long (366 in leap years), it doesn't divide evenly by the seven days of the week.

Also, the Earth goes around the Sun in about 365-1/4 days, so a calendar tends to drift over time. That's why the same date falls on different weekdays in different years.

This is made even more complicated by a change in calendars that took place in 1582. Our modern calendar has its roots in ancient Rome, in a calendar reform conducted by Julius Caesar. Caesar commissioned mathematicians to attack the problem, and they came up with the idea of leap years, and thus standardized the calendar for centuries to come. This was called the Julian calendar.

Over time, however, the small errors in Caesar's calculation compounded. That's why Pope Gregory XIII commissioned the Gregorian calendar, used in most of the world today. Some countries converted in 1582, when the calendar was first developed; some converted later; other still haven't changed.

Gregorian and Julian aren't the only types of calendars. The Hebrew year, the Islamic year, and many other calendars are used in different parts of the world and among different people.

You can convert Gregorian dates to other calendars, including the Hebrew calendar, the Islamic calendar, and even the Mayan calendar by visiting the Fourmilab Calendar Converter at http://www.fourmilab.ch/documents/calendar/.

Chinese calendar systems are quite complex and have changed several times; a full discussion is far beyond the scope of this book. If you're interested, you can find information here: http://www.hermetic.ch/cal_stud/chinese_cal.htm.

On Names and Dates

Historians use "CE" (Common Era) and "BCE" (Before the Common Era) instead of the more common "AD" (Anno Domini, or Year of Our Lord) and "BC" (Before Christ), reflecting the fact that the year-numbering system established by the Gregorian calendar is used throughout the world in many countries not culturally Christian.

The CE/BCE designation dates back to at least 1708, and has been adopted as a standard by the United Nations and the Universal Postal Union. Because this series of books covers events and people of all nations and cultures, we use the CE/BCE terms.

The abbreviation "O.S." ("Old Style") and "N.S." ("New Style") on some dates refers to the fact that the Russian Empire (in particular) did not switch from the Julian to the Gregorian calendar at the same time as the rest of Europe, and therefore some figures and events have two dates.

Also, in the Julian calendar in England in the 16th century, the year began on March 25 rather than January 1. To avoid confusion with Gregorian dates, dates between January and March were often written using both years.

People and events whose original names are not in the Western alphabet have their native names (where possible) in the appropriate script shown in parenthesis. If you are using an e-reader to access an electronic version of this book, all characters don't always display on all devices.

A 50-year brass perpetual calendar.

Quote of the Day

"Time is an illusion, lunchtime doubly so."

Douglas Adams,
from *The Hitchhiker's Guide to the Galaxy*

Notes
and
Credits
Timespinner
Press

Cartoon by John T. McCutcheon

Copyright, Credit, and Contact

Follow Us

Our blog "This Day in History" (http://
timespinnerpress.com/this-day-in-history/) features short
articles on events and people associated with each day, and
updates several times each week. Also subscribe to the
"Quote of the Day" at http://timespinnerpress.com/quote-
of-the-day/. You can get daily links by following us on
Facebook at TimespinnerPress, or on Twitter as
@sidewisethinker.

Contact Us

Find an error or a format problem? Want information about
the series, about us, or about when the volume for your
special day might be available? Please email us at
editor@timespinnerpress.com. (We also take requests if your
special day isn't yet complete. Please give us at least six
weeks' notice if possible.)

Sources

We owe a great debt to Wikipedia, which is our first stop for
research. We attempt to make independent confirmation of
all important dates and facts through a variety of other
sources.

Other sources we frequently use include the Library of
Congress; "on this day" listings from *Encyclopedia Britannica*,
the *New York Times*, and the BBC; Omniglot for the names of
months in other languages; *Chase's Calendar of Events*; and, of
course, the always essential Google.

All art and photographs are either in the public domain, used under a Creative Commons license, or with a "fair use" justification, and most frequently come from Wikimedia Commons and the Library of Congress Prints and Photographs Division.

Attribution is provided where possible, or as requested by the copyright owner, or when there is particular historical significance, listed below. For information about any particular illustration or photograph, please contact us.

Credits

1. The "Chandos portrait" of William Shakespeare was created in 1610 by an artist thought to be John Taylor, and is in the collection of the National Portrait Gallery, London. It is in the public domain because its copyright has expired.

2. The illustration of the month of April used on the back cover is from the French Gothic illuminated manuscript *Les Très Riches Heures du duc de Berry* by the Limbourg Brothers, Jean Colombe, and an intermediate painter whose name is lost to history. It is in the public domain because its copyright has expired.

3. The box graphic used on the first page is from a 1916 pamphlet entitled "Divorce versus Democracy" authored by G. K. Chesterton, originally published in London by the Society of St. Peter and St. Paul. It is in the public domain in the US because it was published prior to 1923, and is in the public domain in all countries (including the country of origin) in which the copyright time is the author's life plus 70 years or less.

4. The graphic design for the section pages in this book is from a design originally created for a pharmacy label. It is courtesy of Wellcome Images (ICV No 11073, photo V0010813), and is used here under CC BY-SA 4.0.

5. The 2014 painting by Alexey Akindinov was made available to the public for free use, and is used here under CC BY-SA 4.0.

6. The wanted poster for John Wilkes Booth is in the public domain because its copyright has expired.

7. The 1826 portrait of John James Audubon by John Syme is in the collection of the White House, Washington, DC. It is in the public domain because its copyright has expired.

8. The cover of the 1623 edition of Shakespeare's First Folio is in the public domain because its copyright has expired.

9. The 2008 photograph of the Globe Theater is by Peter Broster, and is used here under CC BY-SA 2.0.

10. The 1800 painting of Shakespeare by William Blake is in the public domain because its copyright has expired.

11. The 1899 photograph of Sarah Bernhardt as Hamlet is courtesy Library of Congress, digital ID cph.3g06529. It is in the public domain because its copyright has expired.

12. The 2012 photograph of Central Park is by Gigi Alt, and is used here under CC BY-SA 3.0.

13. The 1926 painting of canvas-backed ducks by John James Audubon is courtesy Wellcome Images (ICV 22546), and is used here under CC BY-SA 4.0.

14. The 2007 photograph of a bust of Marcus Aurelius is by Bibi Saint-Pol, who released the work into the public domain without restriction.

15. The 1960 publicity photograph of Bobby Rydell is in the public domain because it was first published in the United States between 1923 and 1977 without a copyright notice. Traditionally, publicity photographs are not copyrighted because of the way in which they are intended to be used.

16. The 1917 photograph of Ma Rainey is in the public domain because its copyright has expired.

17. The 1974 publicity photograph of Carol Burnett is in the public domain because it was first published in the United States between 1923 and 1977 without a copyright notice.

18. The 1954 Toho Company movie poster for *Godzilla* is in the public domain in its country of origin because it is more than 50 years old.

19. The 1953 photograph of Harry Gallatin originally appeared in *The Sporting News*. It is in the public domain because it

was first published in the United States between 1923 and 1977 without a copyright notice.

20. The 1920 photograph of Eddie Eagan is in the public domain because its copyright has expired.

21. The photograph of Count Basie by William Gottlieb is from the William P. Gottlieb Collection at the Library of Congress (digital ID gottlieb.00471). In accordance with the wishes of William Gottlieb, the photographs in this collection entered into the public domain on February 16, 2010.

22. The 1956 publicity photograph from *I Love Lucy* is in the public domain because it was first published in the United States between 1923 and 1977 without a copyright notice.

23. The 1968 photograph of Irene Ryan on *Petticoat Junction* is in the public domain because it was first published in the United States between 1923 and 1977 without a copyright notice. It has been cropped.

24. The 1937 photograph of Gypsy Rose Lee was taken for the Los Angeles *Times*. It is in the public domain because it was published in the United States between 1923 and 1963, and although there may or may not have been a copyright notice, the copyright was not renewed.

25. The painting *La crucifixión* by El Greco is located in the Museo del Prado. It is in the public domain because its copyright has expired.

26. The photograph of Czechoslovakian Easter eggs was taken by Jan Kameníček, who has released the image into the public domain.

27. The 1988 photograph of a Bright Week procession is by George Rassasphore and is used here under the CC BY-SA 1.0 license.

28. The 1563 painting *The First Passover Feast* by Huybrecht Beuckelaer is in the public domain because its copyright has expired.

29. The 2011 photograph of a New Year's pretzel near Heilbronn, Germany, was taken by Rosenzweig, and is used here under CC BY-SA 3.0.

30. The 1896 drawing "April" by Eugène Grasset is in the public domain because its copyright has expired.

31. The painting "April" by Simon Bening is from the *Brevarium Grimani,* circa 1510, and is in the public domain because its copyright has expired.

32. The 1815 woodcut of a proposal is in the public domain because its copyright has expired.

33. The photograph of two diamonds grown by Washington Diamonds was taken by Inbai-Tania Studio, and is used here under the CC BY-SA 3.0 license.

34. The photograph of a daisy (*Bellis perennis*) was taken by André Karwath and is used here under the CC BY-SA 2.5 license.

35. The celestial sphere is from *Scenography of the Ptolemaic Cosmography,* by Johannes van Loon, based on Andreas Cellarius's *Harmonia Macrocosmica,* 1660. It is in the public domain because its copyright has expired.

36. The 1906 automobile calendar is by Edward Penfield, and is in the collection of the Library of Congress Prints and Photographs Division. It is in the public domain because its copyright has expired.

37. The 50-year perpetual calendar photograph is in the public domain.

38. The cartoon by John T. McCutcheon is from his 1905 collection *The Mysterious Stranger and Other Cartoons by John T. McCutcheon.* It is in the public domain because its copyright has expired.

39. The painting "April" by Hans Thoma is from his book *Festkalender.* It is in the public domain because it was published prior to 1923 and its copyright has expired.

License Description and Terms

Aside from material purely in the public domain, photographs and other material in this book are used under specific licenses permitting free use, usually with an attribution requirement. For full text and terms of these licenses, click or enter the appropriate links below. If you believe there is an error in the copyright status or attribution of any of these images, please email us.

- Creative Commons Attribution 2.0 Generic (CC-BY 2.0): http://creativecommons.org/licenses/by/2.0/deed.en
- Creative Commons Attribution-Share Alike 3.0 Generic (CC-BY-SA 3.0): http://creativecommons.org/licenses/by-sa/3.0/
- Creative Commons Attribution-Share Alike 2.5 Generic (CC-BY-SA 2.5): http://creativecommons.org/licenses/by-sa/2.5/deed.en
- Creative Commons Attribution-Share Alike 2.0 Generic (CC-BY-SA 2.0): http://creativecommons.org/licenses/by/2.0/deed.en
- Creative Commons Attribution-Share Alike 1.0 Generic (CC-BY-SA 1.0): http://creativecommons.org/licenses/by-sa/1.0/deed.en
- CC0 1.0 Universal (CC0 1.0) Public Domain Dedication (CC0 1.0) http://creativecommons.org/publicdomain/zero/1.0/deed.en
- GNU Free Documentation License (GFDL): http://en.wikipedia.org/wiki/Wikipedia:Text_of_the_GNU_Free_Documentation_License
- License Art Libre (Free Art License): http://artlibre.org

Other Books from Timespinner Press

The Story of a Special Day

Michael Dobson

A series of (eventually) 366 volumes covering everything that happened on your special day! Events, births, deaths, quotes, holidays, and much more. It's like a birthday card they'll never throw away!

US$7.95 print / US$2.99 ebook.

From Plassey to Pakistan

Humayun Mirza

The history of British Colonial India and the formation of Pakistan from the unique perspective of the son of Pakistan's first president and last of the royal line of Bengal, Bihar, and Orissa! This unique historical document tells the inside story of this distinguished family, including the detailed story of the coup that toppled his father from power!

US$27.95 print

A Whole New Navy: America's War in the Pacific

Miles Durr

The most comprehensive and detailed description of America's naval war in the Pacific ever—every battle, every ship, every task force and every task group from Pearl Harbor through the Japanese surrender! A must-have for the collection of every World War II buff!

US$29.95 print

Improbable History: The Weird, the Obscure, and the Strangely Important

edited by Michael Dobson

From the birth of Western civilization to the rescue of Apollo 13, from the Leaning Tower of Pisa to Florence's Duomo, history has often turned on small, improbable details. Whatever happened to the ancient Samaritan people? Why did a fortuitous rainstorm allow the British to conquer India? How did an air raid in Italy lead to the development of chemotherapy? What happened when Albert Einstein met Adolf Hitler on the streets of Berlin? How did the Japanese manage to attack the US mainland using balloons? A cast of award-winning writers tackle some of the strangest tales in history!

US$19.95 print

The Letters of William Philip Schwartz 1842-1855

edited by John F. Schwartz

The 19th century soldier and adventurer William Philip Schwartz wrote a series of vivid and detailed letters chronicling his adventures in the Indian Wars, the Mexican-American War, the Gold Rush, and his term as Marine sergeant aboard the USS Constellation. A pioneer in photography, he took *the first known war photographs*. An unforgettable first-hand look into life in the 19th century!

US$17.95 print

Timespinner
Press

www.timespinnerpress.com

April, by Hans Thoma